NEPTUNE

BY PAUL FLEISHER

LERNER PUBLICATIONS COMPANY • MINNEAPOLIS

The images in this book are used with the permission of: © NASA/Time & Life Pictures/ Getty Images, pp. 4, 25, 32, 34, 35, 36, 47; © Ludek Pesek/Photo Researchers, Inc., p. 5; © Yoshinori Watabe/Amana Images/Getty Images, p. 6; © Jim Craigmyle/CORBIS, p. 7; © Hulton Archive/Getty Images, pp. 8, 10; NASA/JPL/USGS, pp. 9, 31, 46; © Jason Reed/ Photodisc/Getty Images, pp. 11, 26; © Royal Astronomical Society/Photo Researchers, Inc., p. 12; NASA/JPL, pp. 13, 17, 24 (bottom), 28, 29; © Laura Westlund/Independent Picture Service, pp. 14-15, 19, 20, 27; NASA/GSFC, p. 16; The International Astronomical Union/ Martin Kommesser, p. 18; © Soren Hald/Stone/Getty Images, p. 21; © Mauritius/SuperStock, p. 22; © Pacific Stock/SuperStock, p. 23; © Science Source/Photo Researchers, Inc., p. 24 (top); © Shigemi Numazawa/Atlas Photo Bank/Photo Researchers, Inc., p. 30; © Matt Holman, Harvard-Smithsonian Center for Astrophysics/Getty Images, p. 33; NASA/KSC, p. 37; © Seth Shostak/Photo Researchers, Inc., p. 38; © Bryan Lowry/Alamy, p. 39; NASA/JSC, p. 40; NASA, L. Sromovsky, and P. Fry (University of Wisconsin-Madison), p. 41; © Michael Carroll/ Phototake, Inc./Alamy, p. 42; NASA, p. 43; © Space Frontiers/Hulton Archive/Getty Images, p. 48 (top); © Chris Butler/Photo Researchers, Inc., p. 48 (bottom).

Front Cover: NASA/JPL.

Lerner Publications Company
A division of Lerner Publishing Group, Inc.
241 First Avenue North
Minneapolis, MN 55401 U.S.A.

Website address: www.lernerbooks.com

Library of Congress Cataloging-in-Publication Data

Fleisher, Paul.
    Neptune / by Paul Fleisher.
        p.   cm. — (Early bird astronomy)
    Includes index.
    ISBN 978–0–7613–4155–0 (lib. bdg. : alk. paper)
    1. Neptune (Planet)—Juvenile literature. I. Title.
QB691.F54 2010
    523.48—dc22   2008045439

Manufactured in the United States of America
1 2 3 4 5 6 – BP – 15 14 13 12 11 10

CONTENTS

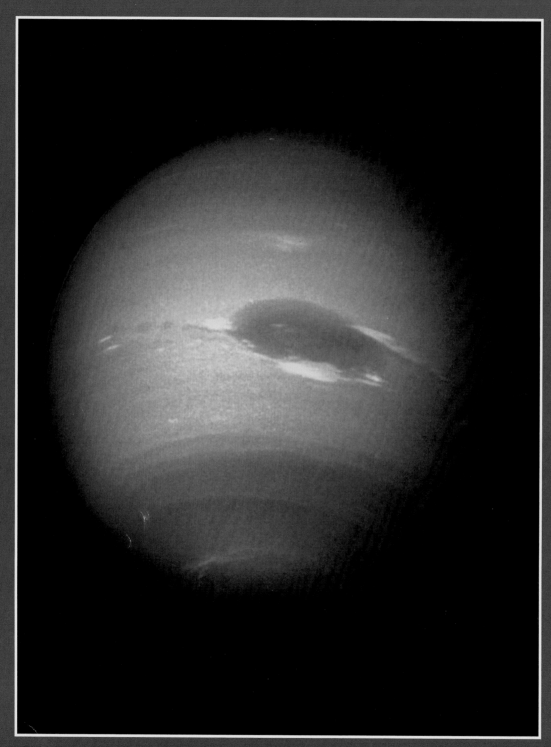

BE A WORD DETECTIVE

Can you find these words as you read about the planet Neptune? Be a detective and try to figure out what they mean. You can turn to the glossary on page 46 for help.

asteroid	elliptical	solar system
astronomers	gravity	spacecraft
atmosphere	orbit	telescope
axis	rotate	

CHAPTER 1
THE MOST DISTANT PLANET

It's a clear, dark night. Stars sparkle in the sky. Among the stars, we see a few planets. They are lit by sunlight. But we can see only the planets that are closest to the Sun. Other planets are much farther away. They don't get as much sunlight. They are too dim for our eyes to see.

The planet Neptune is very far from the Sun. It's very dim. You need a telescope (TEH-luh-skohp) to see it. Telescopes make faraway objects look bigger and closer. With a telescope, Neptune looks like a beautiful blue ball.

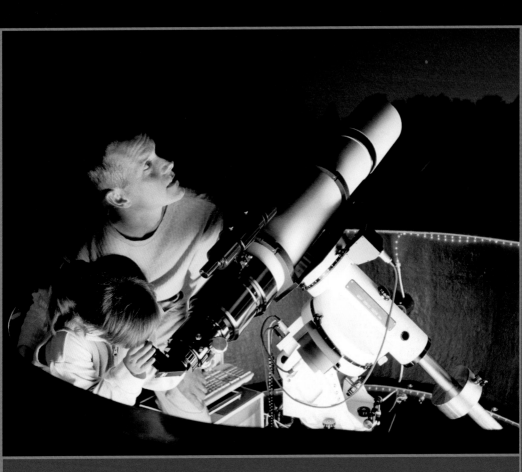

Telescopes help people see stars and planets in the night sky. Objects in space appear closer through a telescope.

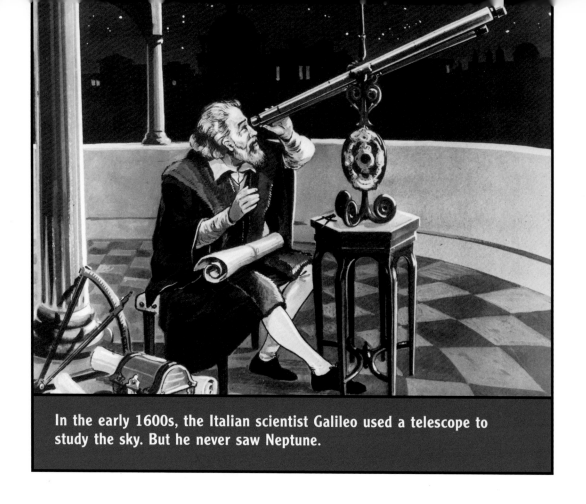

In the early 1600s, the Italian scientist Galileo used a telescope to study the sky. But he never saw Neptune.

Astronomers (uh-STRAH-nuh-murz) didn't see this blue planet for a long time. Astronomers are scientists. They study stars and planets. They study moons and other objects in space. Astronomers have studied planets for thousands of years. But they didn't find Neptune until 1846. It just wasn't bright enough to see.

If Neptune is so dim, how did anyone find it? The planet Uranus (YUR-uh-nuhs) led scientists to Neptune. Uranus was discovered in 1781. Astronomers tracked its path across the sky. Uranus didn't move the way they expected. It seemed to speed up. Then it slowed down. Astronomers wondered why this happened.

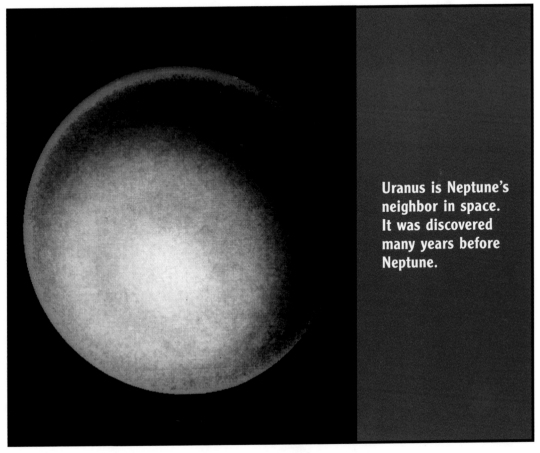

Uranus is Neptune's neighbor in space. It was discovered many years before Neptune.

British astronomer
John Couch Adams
was one of the first to
think there was another
planet past Uranus.

Two people thought they knew. One was a
scientist in Britain. His name was John Couch
Adams. The other was from France. His name
was Urbain Leverrier. They thought there might
be an unknown planet. The planet would be
even farther away than Uranus. They thought its
gravity (GRA-vuh-tee) made Uranus change speed.

All planets have gravity. Gravity is a force. It pulls objects toward one another. When you drop a ball, it falls to the ground. Gravity pulls the ball to Earth.

The gravity of the unknown planet pulled on Uranus. As the planets got closer, the pull made Uranus go faster. When they moved apart, it slowed Uranus down. The two scientists used math. They figured where the mystery planet might be. They told astronomers where to look.

Neptune (LEFT) and Uranus are very far apart in space. This illustration shows how they would look if they were close together. Neptune has a darker blue color.

Johann Galle was the first to find Neptune. Galle was a German astronomer. He saw the planet in 1846. Others had seen this dot through their telescopes. But they didn't know it was a planet. They thought it was a star.

Johann Galle found Neptune in 1846. Several objects in space have been named after him.

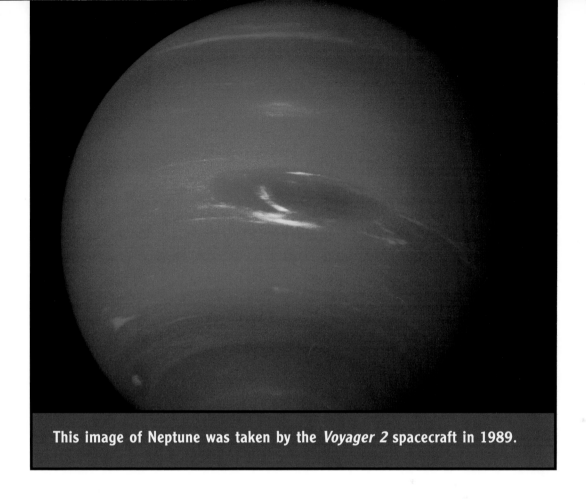

This image of Neptune was taken by the *Voyager 2* spacecraft in 1989.

Modern scientists use spacecraft to learn more about planets. Spacecraft are machines that travel from Earth to outer space. They take pictures and send back information. Only one spacecraft has visited Neptune. It was named *Voyager 2*. It taught us much of what we know about Neptune.

Kuiper belt

Pluto

Neptune

Uranus

Saturn

Jupiter

CHAPTER 2
NEPTUNE'S NEIGHBORHOOD

Neptune and Earth are both part of the solar system. The solar system includes the Sun and eight planets. It also has dwarf planets. They are smaller than the eight main planets. Other smaller objects are in the solar system too. These include rocks called asteroids (A-stur-oydz).

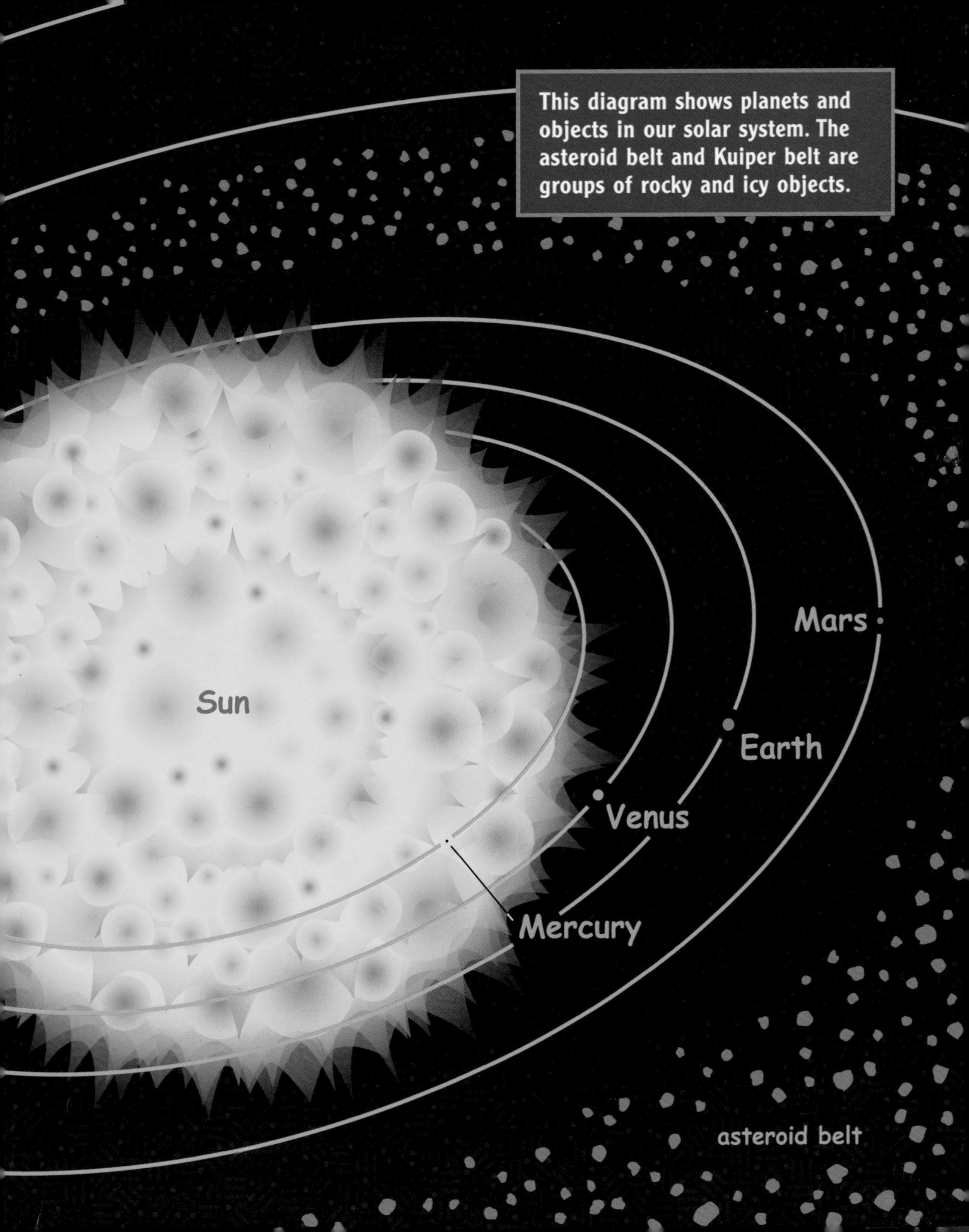

This diagram shows planets and objects in our solar system. The asteroid belt and Kuiper belt are groups of rocky and icy objects.

Mars

Earth

Sun

Venus

Mercury

asteroid belt

The Sun is the center of the solar system. The planets closest to the Sun are Mercury and Venus. Earth is the third planet from the Sun. Then comes Mars. These four planets are made mostly of rock. Scientists call them the rocky planets.

Earth's land and ocean floors are made of rock.

Neptune, Uranus, Saturn, and Jupiter (LEFT TO RIGHT) are gas planets. They are much larger than the rocky planets.

The next planets are Jupiter and Saturn. Beyond them is Uranus. Finally, there's Neptune. These four planets are made mostly of gas. They are called gas giants. They are much larger than the rocky planets.

Neptune is the smallest gas giant. But it's *much* larger than Earth. About 58 Earths could fit inside Neptune.

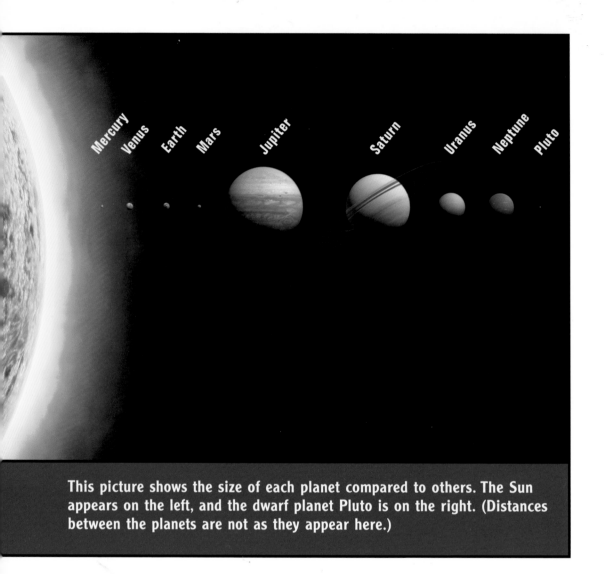

This picture shows the size of each planet compared to others. The Sun appears on the left, and the dwarf planet Pluto is on the right. (Distances between the planets are not as they appear here.)

Planets are always moving. Each follows its own curved path around the Sun. The paths are called orbits. Each orbit is elliptical (ih-LIHP-tih-kuhl). That means it's oval shaped.

Neptune is the farthest planet from the Sun. Its orbit is huge. Neptune orbits almost 3 billion miles (4.5 billion kilometers) from the Sun.

Neptune's orbit is much larger than Earth's. So it takes much more time to circle the Sun. Earth orbits the Sun in one year. Neptune's orbit takes almost 165 Earth years.

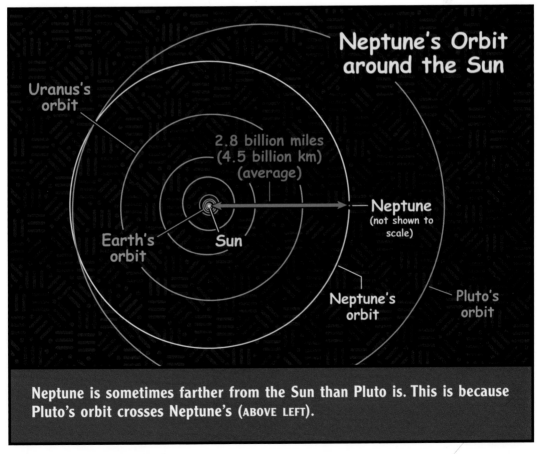

Neptune's Orbit around the Sun

Uranus's orbit

2.8 billion miles (4.5 billion km) (average)

Earth's orbit

Sun

Neptune (not shown to scale)

Neptune's orbit

Pluto's orbit

Neptune is sometimes farther from the Sun than Pluto is. This is because Pluto's orbit crosses Neptune's (ABOVE LEFT).

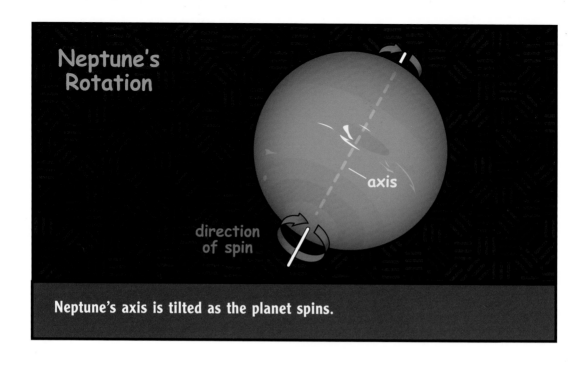

Neptune's Rotation

axis

direction of spin

Neptune's axis is tilted as the planet spins.

As planets travel, they also rotate (ROH-tayt). That means they spin like a top. A planet rotates on its axis (AK-sihs). An axis is an imaginary line through the center of the planet. Neptune's axis is slightly tilted.

Neptune spins very fast. It takes only about 16 hours and 7 minutes to rotate once. A rotation equals one day on the planet. Earth takes 24 hours to rotate. So a day on Neptune is shorter than a day on Earth.

Neptune's fast rotation changes its shape. Spinning makes the planet bulge in the middle. The same thing happens when someone twirls in a skirt. Spinning makes the skirt fly out into the air. Neptune's bulge makes it look like a flattened ball.

Twirling makes this ice skater's skirt fly away from her body. The same motion makes Neptune's center bulge.

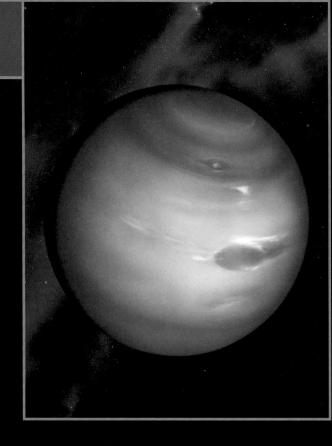

Neptune looks like a blue ball in space. What gives Neptune its blue color?

CHAPTER 3

A BLUE BALL OF GAS

What would it be like to step onto Neptune? Impossible! Earth has a solid surface. You can stand on it. Neptune is mostly gas. There's nothing to stand on.

The layer of gases that surrounds a planet is called the atmosphere (AT-muhs-feer). We call Earth's atmosphere air. We breathe oxygen in the air.

On Neptune, the atmosphere makes up much of the planet. This thick layer of gas is mostly hydrogen (HY-druh-jehn). It has some helium (HEE-lee-uhm) too. Neptune's atmosphere also has methane (MEH-thayn) gas. Methane gives Neptune its blue color. People could not breathe Neptune's gases.

Earth's atmosphere surrounds the planet's solid surface. Neptune's atmosphere blends into the planet itself.

Light-colored clouds float in Neptune's outer atmosphere. *Voyager 2* took pictures of them. The clouds are probably frozen methane. Other clouds might be water ice.

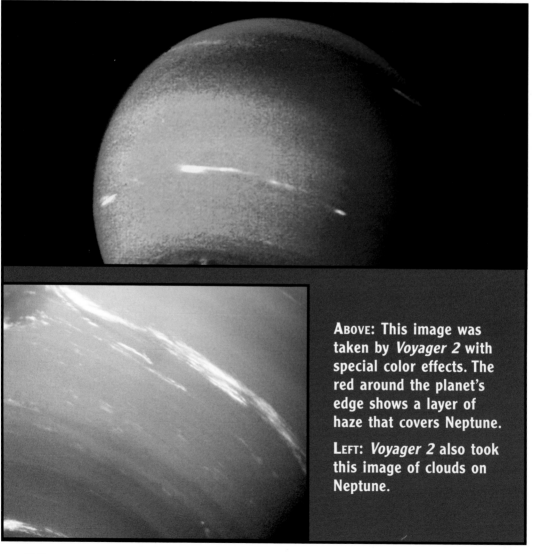

ABOVE: This image was taken by *Voyager 2* with special color effects. The red around the planet's edge shows a layer of haze that covers Neptune.

LEFT: *Voyager 2* also took this image of clouds on Neptune.

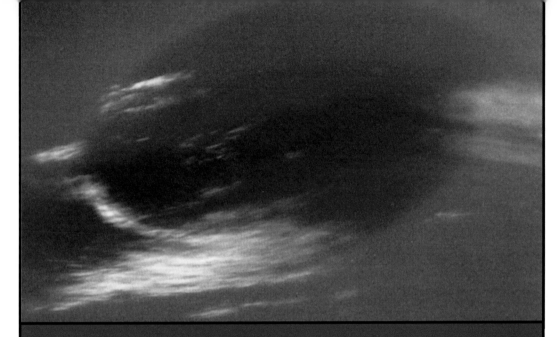

This close-up image shows the storm on Neptune known as the Great Dark Spot. *Voyager 2* photographed the storm in 1989.

Fast winds blow the clouds around the planet. Neptune has the strongest winds of any planet. The wind can blow at speeds up to 1,570 miles (2,520 km) per hour. The wind helps create storms. *Voyager 2* found a storm that looked like a dark blue spot. This storm was huge. It was as wide as Earth! Several years later, the storm had disappeared, but other storms had formed.

Neptune is very cold. Very little of the Sun's heat reaches it. The temperature of its outer layers is about −353°F (−214°C).

Suppose you traveled to the center of Neptune. As you went deeper, the gas in the atmosphere would get thicker. Neptune's inner layers are probably liquid. They may be frozen.

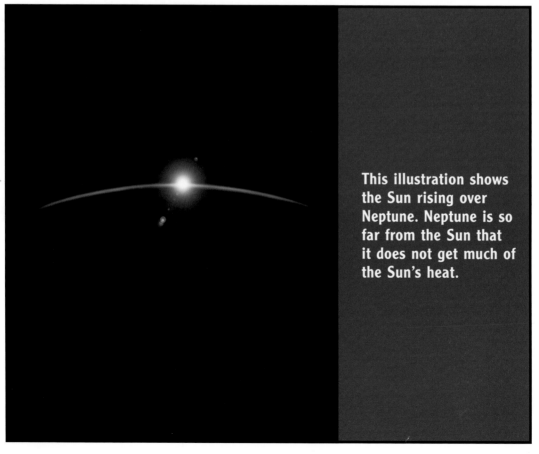

This illustration shows the Sun rising over Neptune. Neptune is so far from the Sun that it does not get much of the Sun's heat.

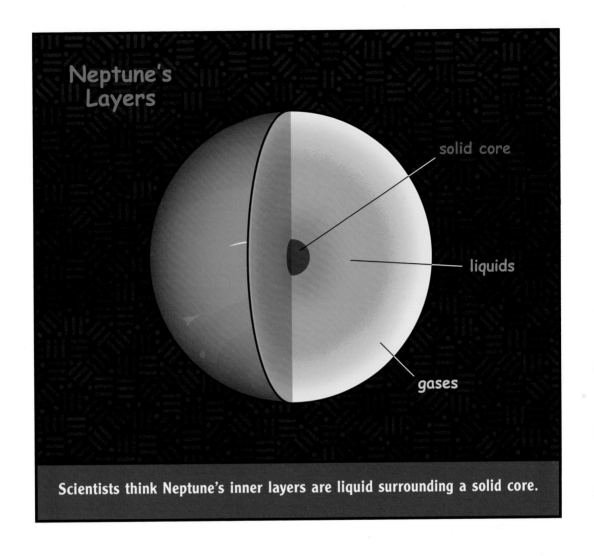

Neptune's
Layers

solid core

liquids

gases

Scientists think Neptune's inner layers are liquid surrounding a solid core.

The center of Neptune is probably hot. Other planets have cores of hot rock and metal. The center of a planet is very dense and heavy. Neptune's center may be like that too. But no one knows for sure.

Neptune is seen here with its largest moon, Triton (BOTTOM RIGHT). How did scientists first see Triton up close?

CHAPTER 4

NEPTUNE'S MOONS AND RINGS

Scientists have discovered 13 moons around Neptune. Triton (TRY-tuhn) is the largest. It is much bigger than Neptune's other moons. Triton is almost as big as Earth's moon.

Voyager 2 took photos of Triton. The photos gave scientists their first close-up view of this moon. Part of it looks like a melon rind. White fountains erupt from the surface. They shoot 5 miles (8 km) high. They may be fountains of liquid nitrogen and methane. The liquids freeze as they rise above the surface. Triton is even colder than Neptune.

Triton is the coldest object that has been measured in the solar system. Its surface is −391°F (−235°C).

Triton is an unusual moon. All moons orbit their planet. But most move in the same direction the planet spins. Triton orbits in the opposite direction. Neptune rotates west to east. But Triton travels east to west.

Triton (LOWER RIGHT) orbits in the opposite direction from Neptune's rotation. Scientists call this a retrograde direction.

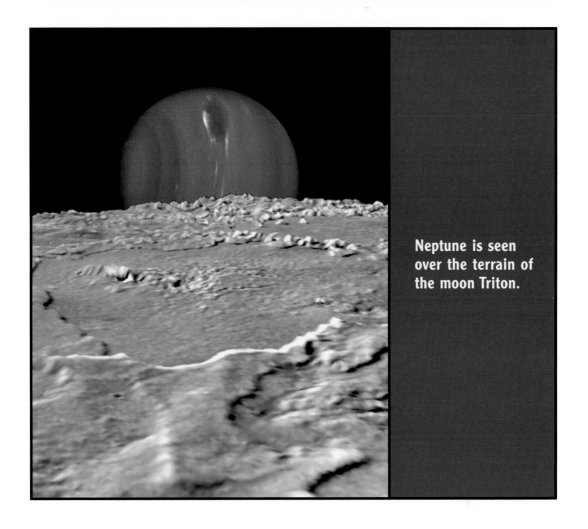

Neptune is seen over the terrain of the moon Triton.

How did this happen? Scientists think Triton wasn't always a moon. Maybe it was a dwarf planet. As it traveled through space, it passed near Neptune. Neptune's gravity caught it. The gravity pulled Triton into orbit around Neptune. Triton became a moon.

Nereid (NEER-ee-ihd) is Neptune's third-largest moon. It was first seen in 1949. Astronomers using telescopes saw it from Earth. *Voyager 2* found six more moons. It found Neptune's second-largest moon, Proteus (PROH-tee-uhs). Proteus is very dark. Its surface doesn't reflect sunlight very well. So it is very hard to see from Earth.

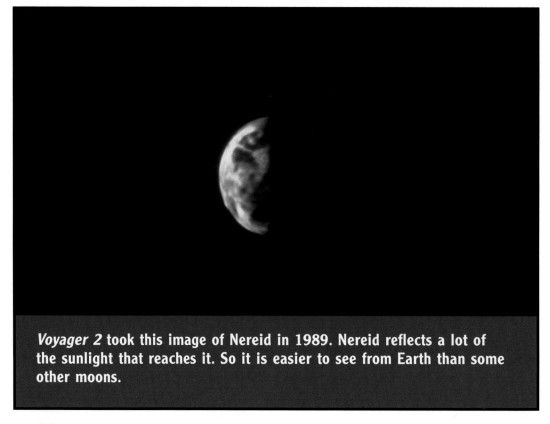

Voyager 2 took this image of Nereid in 1989. Nereid reflects a lot of the sunlight that reaches it. So it is easier to see from Earth than some other moons.

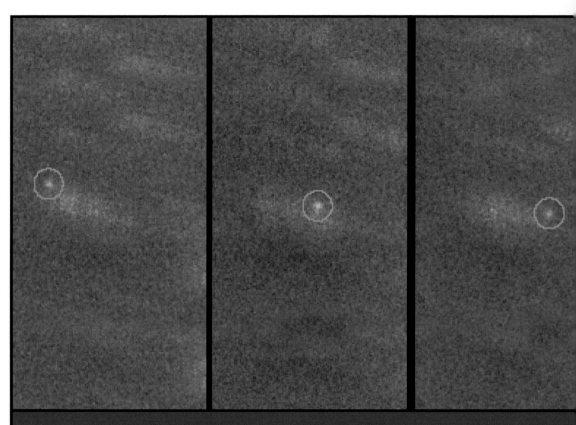

These three moons (CIRCLED IN GREEN) orbiting Neptune were discovered in 2003. These were the first moons around Neptune discovered from a ground-based telescope since 1949.

Astronomers kept looking for moons. They built better telescopes to get clearer views of space. By the end of 2003, they saw several more moons around Neptune. So far, they've found 13 moons. But there may be others.

Neptune also has rings. The rings are made of bits of rock and dust. The rocks and dust orbit the planet like a moon.

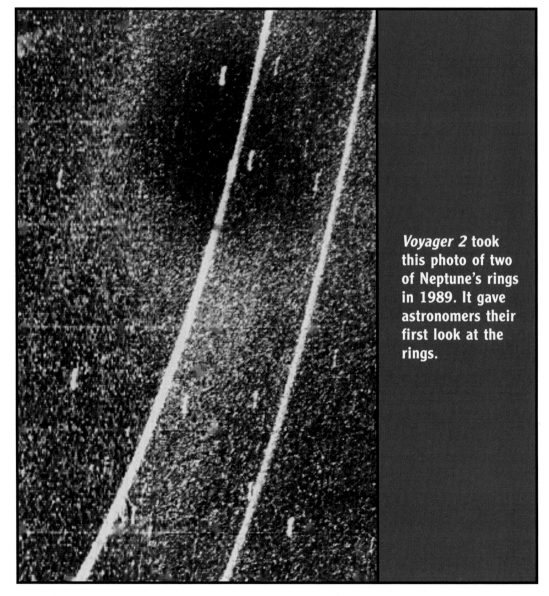

Voyager 2 took this photo of two of Neptune's rings in 1989. It gave astronomers their first look at the rings.

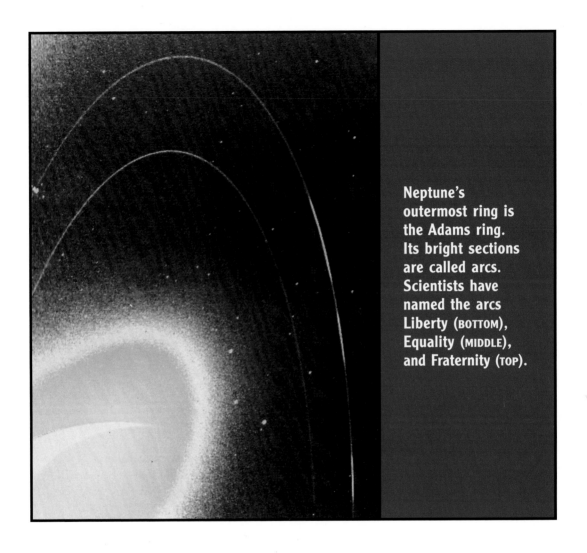

Neptune's outermost ring is the Adams ring. Its bright sections are called arcs. Scientists have named the arcs Liberty (BOTTOM), Equality (MIDDLE), and Fraternity (TOP).

Neptune's rings are very thin. They aren't as bright as Saturn's. They aren't as colorful. No one noticed them for a long time. *Voyager 2* took the first pictures of the rings when it flew past the planet. It sent the photos back to Earth.

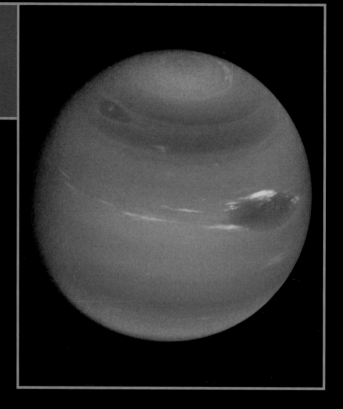

This image of Neptune was taken by the spacecraft that flew by Neptune in 1989. What was the name of that spacecraft?

CHAPTER 5
A VOYAGE TO NEPTUNE

Without *Voyager 2*, we would know much less about Neptune. Neptune is just too far away. From Earth, telescopes can't get a clear, close-up look at the planet. To learn more, scientists needed a closer view.

Voyager 2 was launched in 1977. The spacecraft had a very long trip ahead of it. It flew past other planets. It traveled through the solar system for 12 years. Then, in 1989, it flew past Neptune.

Voyager 2 lifted off in 1977. It visited Jupiter, Saturn, Uranus, and Neptune.

Voyager 2 took about 10,000 pictures around Neptune. It took pictures of the planet. It took pictures of Neptune's moons and rings. Scientists were amazed by all the new information it sent back to Earth.

This illustration shows *Voyager 2* flying by Neptune. The Sun is shown in the distance (UPPER RIGHT). The spacecraft continued into the outer solar system.

W. M. Keck Observatory in Hawaii has two of the largest telescopes in the world. The observatory is on top of a mountain. Earth's atmosphere is thinner there. That gives the telescopes clearer views of space.

People still study Neptune with telescopes too. Huge, powerful telescopes take photos of Neptune and its neighborhood in space. Scientists used computers to combine some of these photos. They discovered five of Neptune's moons this way. *Voyager 2* hadn't taken pictures of those moons. They were too small and dim for it to find.

The Hubble Space Telescope helps astronomers study many things in space that are hard to see from Earth's surface.

Astronomers also study Neptune using the Hubble Space Telescope. This telescope is a spacecraft. It was launched in 1990. It orbits Earth.

Astronomers using telescopes on Earth's surface must see through the atmosphere. The air makes it hard to see clearly. But the Hubble Space Telescope is outside Earth's atmosphere. It can take much clearer pictures.

The Hubble telescope takes pictures of planets and stars. These pictures have helped scientists learn about Neptune's atmosphere. They show Neptune's weather changing very quickly. They also tell us that Neptune probably has four seasons.

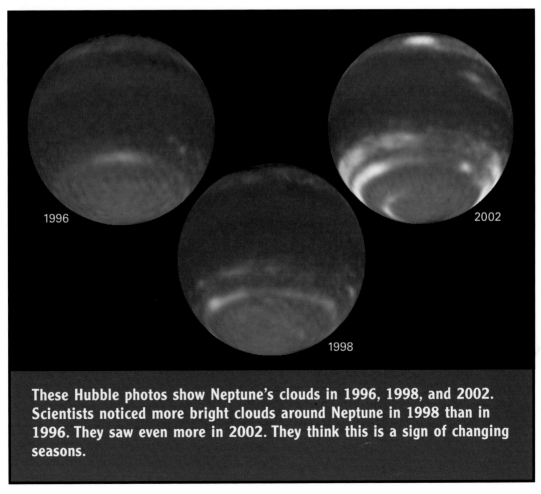

1996

2002

1998

These Hubble photos show Neptune's clouds in 1996, 1998, and 2002. Scientists noticed more bright clouds around Neptune in 1998 than in 1996. They saw even more in 2002. They think this is a sign of changing seasons.

Scientists still want to know more about Neptune. They want to send another spacecraft there. Some people have begun to plan the flight. This new spacecraft would orbit Neptune. It would study the planet and its moons.

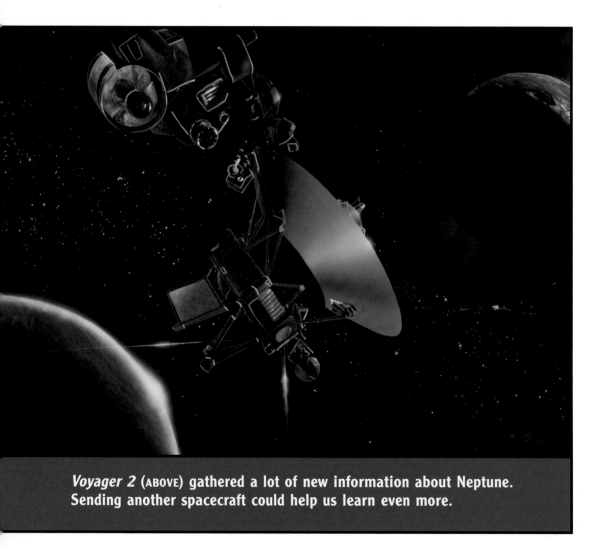

Voyager 2 (ABOVE) gathered a lot of new information about Neptune. Sending another spacecraft could help us learn even more.

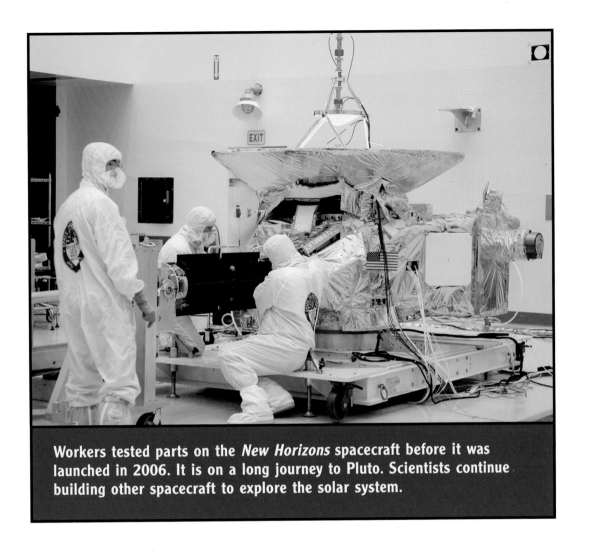

Workers tested parts on the *New Horizons* spacecraft before it was launched in 2006. It is on a long journey to Pluto. Scientists continue building other spacecraft to explore the solar system.

A new spacecraft wouldn't leave Earth for several years. It wouldn't reach Neptune before 2035. You'll be old enough to help with this spacecraft. Maybe you could be an astronomer. You could help learn more about Neptune.

ON SHARING A BOOK

When you share a book with a child, you show that reading is important. To get the most out of the experience, read in a comfortable, quiet place. Turn off the television and limit other distractions, such as telephone calls. Be prepared to start slowly. Take turns reading parts of this book. Stop occasionally and discuss what you're reading. Talk about the photographs. If the child begins to lose interest, stop reading. When you pick up the book again, revisit the parts you have already read.

BE A VOCABULARY DETECTIVE

The word list on page 5 contains words that are important in understanding the topic of this book. Be word detectives and search for the words as you read the book together. Talk about what the words mean and how they are used in the sentence. Do any of these words have more than one meaning? You will find the words defined in a glossary on page 46.

WHAT ABOUT QUESTIONS?

Use questions to make sure the child understands the information in this book. Here are some suggestions:

What did this paragraph tell us? What does this picture show? What do you think we'll learn about next? Which planets are gas giants? What is the name of Neptune's biggest moon? Which gases make up Neptune? Why is it hard to see Neptune from Earth? What is your favorite part of the book? Why?

If the child has questions, don't hesitate to respond with questions of your own, such as What do *you* think? Why? What is it that you don't know? If the child can't remember certain facts, turn to the index.

INTRODUCING THE INDEX

The index helps readers find information without searching through the whole book. Turn to the index on page 48. Choose an entry such as *telescope,* and ask the child to use the index to find out how telescopes help astronomers. Repeat with as many entries as you like. Ask the child to point out the differences between an index and a glossary. (The index helps readers find information, while the glossary tells readers what words mean.)

NEPTUNE

BOOKS

Landau, Elaine. *Neptune*. New York: Children's Press, 2008. This title includes general information and interesting facts about Neptune, its moons, and its rings.

Ride, Sally, and Tam O'Shaughnessy. *Voyager: An Adventure to the Edge of the Solar System*. New York: Crown Publishers, 1992. Read more about the *Voyager* spacecraft and their long trips past Jupiter, Saturn, Uranus, and Neptune in this book by astronaut Sally Ride.

Rudy, Lisa Jo, and editors of *TIME for Kids. Planets!* New York: HarperCollins, 2005. Make a visit to each of the planets in our solar system in this book.

Simon, Seymour. *Our Solar System*. Rev. Ed. New York: Collins, 2007. This overview of the solar system features vivid photos and colorful illustrations.

WEBSITES

The Hubble Site gallery
http://hubblesite.org/gallery/album/
Check out tons of photos taken by the Hubble Space Telescope!

NASA SpacePlace
http://spaceplace.nasa.gov/en/kids/
NASA's website for kids has activities, quizzes, and games about outer space.

Neptune: Kid's Eye View
http://solarsystem.nasa.gov/planets/profile
.cfm?Object=Neptune&Display=Kids
Find out how much you would weigh on Neptune! This NASA website also has facts and links to help you learn more.

GLOSSARY

asteroid (A-stur-oyd): a rocky body, much smaller than a planet, that orbits the Sun

astronomers (uh-STRAH-nuh-murz): scientists who study outer space

atmosphere (AT-muhs-feer): the layer of gases that surrounds a planet

axis (AK-sihs): an imaginary line through the center of a planet. A planet spins on its axis.

elliptical (ih-LIHP-tih-kuhl): oval shaped

gravity (GRA-vuh-tee): a force that pulls objects toward each other

orbit: path of a planet, moon, or other object in space. *Orbit* can also mean to move along this path.

rotate (ROH-tayt): to spin around like a top

solar system: the group of planets and other objects that travel around the Sun

spacecraft: machines that travel from Earth to outer space

telescope (TEH-luh-skohp): an instrument that makes faraway objects look bigger and closer

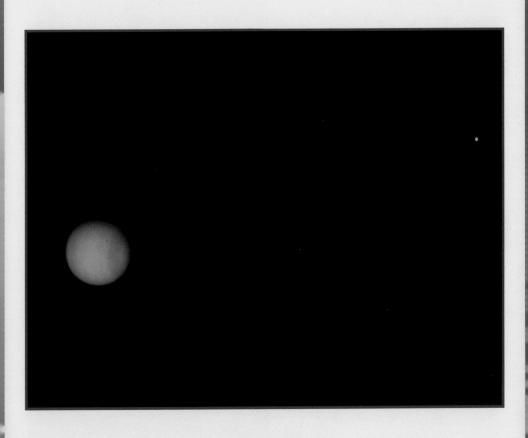

INDEX

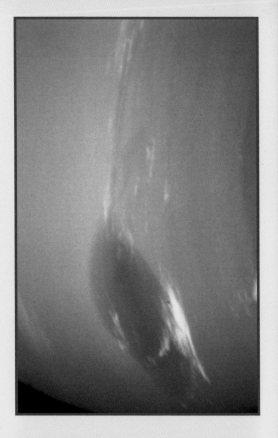